Easter

Katie Dicker

WAYLAND

First published in 2007 by Wayland
Copyright © Wayland 2007

Wayland
338 Euston Road
London NW1 3BH

Wayland Australia
Level 17/207 Kent Street
Sydney NSW 2000

Produced for Wayland by

White-Thomson Publishing Ltd.
210 High Street,
Lewes BN7 2NH

Editor: Katie Dicker
Designer: Clare Nicholas
Picture research: Amy Sparks
Editorial consultant: Sian Williams

Picture credits
The publishers would like to thank the following for reproducing these photographs: Front cover main, 20 – www.photolibrary.com/Foodpix. Front cover inset, 26 – © Tristan da Cunha/Alamy. 3, 7 – © Rick Gomez/Corbis. 6 – © Ajay Verma/Reuters/Corbis. 8 – The Bridgeman Art Library. 9 – © Martin Rogers/Corbis. 10 – www.istockphoto.com/James Margolis. 11 – Giraudon/The Bridgeman Art Library. 12 – www.istockphoto.com/Rob Sylvan. 13 – www.istockphoto.com/Chris Johnson. 14 – © Ariel Skelley/Corbis. 15 – © Hemis/Alamy. 16 – © Chuck Savage/Corbis. 17 – © Todd Muskopf/Alamy. 18 – © World Religions Photo Library/Alamy. 19 – The Bridgeman Art Library. 21 – www.istockphoto.com/Will Iredale. 22 – www.photolibrary.com/Tim Hill. 23 – www.photolibrary.com/Imagestate Ltd. 24 – www.istockphoto.com/Nico Smit. 25 – www.istockphoto.com/Mario Hornik. 27 – © Martin Harvey; Gallo Images/Corbis.

British Library Cataloguing in Publication Data
Dicker, Katie
    Easter. - (Special Days of the Year)
    1. Easter - Juvenile literature
    I. Title
    394.2'667

ISBN 978 0 7502 5234 8

Printed in China

Wayland is a division of Hachette Children's Books, an Hachette Livre UK company.

Note: The website addresses (URLs) included in this book were valid at the time of going to press. However, because of the nature of the Internet, it is possible that some addresses may have changed, or sites may have changed or closed down since publication. While the authors and publishers regret any inconvenience this may cause readers, no responsibility for any such changes can be accepted by either the authors or the publisher.

Contents

What are special days?

We use special days to celebrate or remember an important time each year. Special days can be important to a person, a family, a town or even a country.

These children from India are lighting candles as part of a Divali celebration.

6

Different religions have special days that are remembered or celebrated. Hindu people, for example, celebrate Divali. This is a festival of light that lasts for five days. One special festival for **Christian** people is called Easter.

Easter is a Christian celebration. These children are painting eggs as part of the festivities.

Christians believe that Jesus was God made man who lived on Earth over 2,000 years ago. Christians think that when Jesus died, he came back to life again. At Easter, they celebrate this miracle.

Jesus helped people who were sick to get better. In this painting, a group of people have gathered to see if Jesus can heal them.

Jesus taught people about God. He also told people to love one another. Although Jesus was killed, Christians believe that he rose from the dead and then went to heaven.

Jesus is sometimes called 'the light of the world'. Christians light candles to remind them of Jesus, especially at Easter.

The Easter story

The Easter story is found in a special book called the Bible. The story describes the last days of Jesus' life. The religious leaders of the time did not like what Jesus was saying about God so they arrested and killed him.

The people who wanted to kill Jesus nailed him on a cross to die. This is a statue showing what happened. We call this type of statue a crucifix.

Jesus' body was taken down from the cross and buried in a special **tomb** in a cave. But afterwards, lots of people said they saw Jesus. His closest friends believed that God had brought him back to life.

In this painting, Jesus is shown rising from the dead three days after he was buried in a tomb. The soldiers guarding the tomb are very shocked.

✝ When is Easter?

Christians celebrate Easter in March or April. The date changes every year because it is linked to the position of the moon.

Easter Sunday is the first Sunday after a full moon in March or April. This is when the moon can be seen as a full circle.

The Friday before Easter is called Good Friday. This is the day that Jesus died on a cross. The main Easter celebrations are on Easter Sunday. On this day, Christians remember that Jesus came alive again.

Easter time is a holiday in many countries.

Easter is a time when Christians think about new life and new beginnings. Families get together to celebrate. At Easter, many families also eat special food, such as eggs, chocolate and hot cross buns.

This family is having a special meal together at Easter.

Christians go to church services at Easter to remember the fact that Jesus came back to life. People say prayers and sing special songs. At Easter, people also send Easter cards, decorate eggs or give chocolates to each other.

There are many church services at Easter time. The churches are decorated with lots of flowers.

✝ Lent

Easter comes after a time called **Lent**. This is when Christians get ready for Easter. During Lent, Christians also remember that Jesus went into the desert for 40 days with little food. He did this to show that he was prepared to suffer to teach people about God.

Many people stop eating their favourite foods during the 40 days of Lent. These children are making pancakes – a traditional food eaten before Lent begins.

The first day of Lent is called Ash Wednesday. On this day, Christians think about the wrong things they have done. Ash is used as a **symbol** of death and of asking for forgiveness.

At this Ash Wednesday church service, ash is being put on people's foreheads in the shape of a cross.

✝ Holy Week

The week before Easter is called Holy Week. This is when Christians remember the last days of Jesus' life. The Sunday before Easter is called Palm Sunday. Christians are reminded of the day when crowds of people went to meet Jesus in Jerusalem. Jesus rode on a donkey and people put palm leaves at his feet.

Christians use these palm crosses to remember the day that Jesus was welcomed by crowds of people in Jerusalem.

The Thursday before Easter is called
Maundy Thursday. This is when Christians
think about the last meal that Jesus had
with his closest friends. This meal is
known as the Last Supper.

Jesus shared
a meal with his
friends on the
night before
he died.

Easter symbols

In many countries, Easter is in the spring. At this time of year, plants and flowers begin to grow and some animals hatch from eggs. Eggs have become a symbol of new beginnings. Christians use eggs to remember their belief that Jesus came back from the dead.

People often give chocolate eggs to each other. We call them Easter eggs.

Another Easter symbol is the cross.
Christians use a cross to remind them
of the way that Jesus died. A cross is also
used throughout the year as a symbol of
Christian beliefs.

A cross is a
symbol found in all
Christian churches.

# Easter food

On Good Friday, many people eat hot cross buns. These buns have a cross on the top made from icing or dough.

Hot cross buns are marked with a cross as a symbol of Easter.

'Hot cross buns are the highlight of Good Friday in our family! We like to eat them with lots of butter.'

Mark

A lot of people also eat boiled eggs on Easter Sunday. Sometimes people colour these eggs with pens or paints. The bright colours are a symbol of the sunlight and flowers in spring. A special cake called a simnel cake is sometimes baked for tea.

A simnel cake has eleven balls of marzipan on the top to represent Jesus' eleven good friends, whom he called his disciples (or apostles).

The Easter bunny

Thousands of years ago, people thought that the hare was an animal that did not close its eyes at night. People used the hare as a symbol for the moon.

Easter falls around the time of a full moon. Because hares are linked with the moon, some people also use them as a symbol of Easter.

Rabbits look like hares and have become a symbol of Easter, too. Rabbits remind us of new life because they have lots of babies in the spring. Today, the symbol of a rabbit or a hare at Easter is described as the Easter Bunny.

Some children think that the eggs they receive come from the Easter Bunny. This rabbit has been made from straw as an Easter gift.

Easter around the world

Easter is celebrated in lots of countries because Christians live around the world. Some countries have their own **traditions**. In Spain and Mexico, for example, lots of people gather in the streets wearing costumes during the last week of Lent.

In Mexico, Easter celebrations last for two weeks.

'In Mexico, it is very busy in the week before Easter. We dress up in colourful costumes and we make special decorations with flowers.'

Gabriela

A lot of Easter symbols are linked to spring time. However, in Australia and New Zealand, Easter comes in the autumn. Whatever the season, Easter celebrations are combined with a holiday in many countries.

In Australia, a bilby is used instead of a rabbit as an Easter symbol. A bilby is a rodent. It has long ears like a rabbit, but it also has a long nose!

 # Glossary and activities

Glossary

Christians – People who follow the teachings of Jesus.

Lent – A time of preparation for Easter.

Rodent – A type of animal, like a mouse, that has large front teeth.

Symbol – A picture or an object that makes us think of something else.

Tomb – A place where someone is buried when they have died.

Tradition – Something people have been doing for hundreds of years.

Books to read

• *The Easter Story* (Usborne Bible Tales) by Heather Amery (Usborne Publishing 2006)

• *The Easter Story* (Festival Stories) by Anita Ganeri (Evans Brothers 2003)

• *Easter* (Celebrations) by Anita Ganeri (Heinemann 2002)

• *The Easter Story* by Lois Rock (Lion Hudson 2002)

• *The Easter Story* by Brian Wildsmith (Eerdmans Books for Young Readers 2000)

Activities

1. Use books or ask an adult to help you use the internet to find out more about the Easter story.
2. Do you celebrate Easter? What special things do your family do each year?
3. Make an Easter card that illustrates part of the Easter story.
4. Make an Easter bonnet.
5. Help your mum or dad to make some Easter biscuits.
6. Decorate some hard-boiled eggs with coloured pens or paints.
7. Use books or ask an adult to help you use the internet to find out what the day before Ash Wednesday is called. Why is this day special?

Useful websites

http://www.bbc.co.uk/schools/religion/christianity/easter.shtml
http://www.topmarks.co.uk/easter
http://www.holidays.net/easter/story.htm

† Index